Stories of the First
Christmas

Brian Miller

ISBN 979-8-89130-258-7 (paperback)
ISBN 979-8-89130-259-4 (digital)

Christian Faith Publishing
832 Park Avenue
Meadville, PA 16335
www.christianfaithpublishing.com

Printed in the United States of America

CONTENTS

Illustrations 1

Introduction...3

Chapter 1   Zacharias...5
Chapter 2   Gabriel Appears to Zacharias.....................9
Chapter 3   Doubt Creeps In 11
Chapter 4   The People Wait Outside 15
Chapter 5   Elisabeth and Zacharias...........................19
Chapter 6   Elisabeth with Child 23
Chapter 7   Mary...27
Chapter 8   Gabriel Appears to Mary..........................31
Chapter 9   The Mother of the Messiah.......................33
Chapter 10   Mary Tells Joseph....................................37
Chapter 11   The Angel Appears to Joseph 43
Chapter 12   Mary and Joseph.....................................49
Chapter 13   Mary Visits Elisabeth 53
Chapter 14   "His Name Is John!" 59
Chapter 15   From Nazareth to Bethlehem 63
Chapter 16   No Room in the Inn 67
Chapter 17   The Saviour is Born 71
Chapter 18   Shepherds in the Field.............................75
Chapter 19   The Angel Visits the Shepherds.................81
Chapter 20   Finding the Saviour.................................85
Chapter 21   Is the Saviour Your Saviour? 91

ILLUSTRATIONS

Zacharias in the Temple
Gabriel Appears to Zacharias
Zacharias Outside with the People
Elisabeth and Zacharias in Their Home
Elisabeth with Child
Mary in the Kitchen
Gabriel Appears to Mary
Joseph Visits Mary
The Angel Appears to Joseph
Joseph Tells Mary about the Angel's Visit
Mary Visits Elisabeth
The Ceremony with the Priests
Traveling from Nazareth to Bethlehem
No Room in the Inn
Jesus, Mary, and Joseph in the Stable
The Shepherd Boy Playing
The Angel Visits the Shepherds
Seeing Jesus

INTRODUCTION

The story of the first Christmas is really a series of events of God working mightily in the lives of ordinary people. This book is a dramatization of events, based on Scripture, surrounding our Saviour's birth.

No matter your age, may your love for the Christmas story and the Saviour be helped, and may your Christmas season be all the more meaningful and joyful by reading and enjoying this book.

All Scriptures are from the King James Bible.

CHAPTER 1

Zacharias

There was in the days of Herod, the king of Judaea, a certain priest named Zacharias, of the course of Abia: and his wife was of the daughters of Aaron, and her name was Elisabeth.

And they were both righteous before God, walking in all the commandments and ordinances of the Lord blameless.

And they had no child, because that Elisabeth was barren, and they both were now well stricken in years.

And it came to pass, that while he executed the priest's office before God in the order of his course, According to the custom of the priest's office, his lot was to burn incense when he went into the temple of the Lord. (Luke 1:5–9)

The temple was quiet and solemn. Zacharias stood alone before the incense altar. He knew it was an honor to serve the Lord as a priest. The temple to him was a special place, a sanctuary from the troubles of the world. It was a place where he especially sensed God's presence.

It also reminded him of a favorite passage:

> *Honour and majesty are before him: strength*
> *and beauty are in his sanctuary. (Psalm 96:6)*

Zacharias placed the incense on the coals. It gave a unique, pleasing scent as the smoke wisped slowly upward. Incense represented prayer. People were outside the temple praying while Zacharias was inside offering incense. Zacharias thought of another favorite passage:

> *O thou that hearest prayer, unto thee shall*
> *all flesh come. (Psalm 65:2)*

God calls Himself the One who hears prayer. Zacharias believed God did hear and answer prayer, though at times he wondered. He and Elisabeth had prayed for many years for a child. Yet they were now elderly and childless.

CHAPTER 2

Gabriel Appears to Zacharias

And there appeared unto him an angel of the Lord standing on the right side of the altar of incense. And when Zacharias saw him, he was troubled, and fear fell upon him. (Luke 1:11–12)

As Zacharias pondered and watched the incense ascend, he suddenly jumped. A man appeared next to the altar: a huge, powerful-looking man in a shining white garment. Zacharias' heart jumped in fear. The man spoke:

Fear not, Zacharias: for thy prayer is heard; and thy wife Elisabeth shall bear thee a son, and thou shalt call his name John. (Luke 1:13)

Who is this man? Zacharias thought. *And how does he know me? And did he say my prayer was heard, and I would have a son?*

The man spoke again:

> *And thou shalt have joy and gladness; and many shall rejoice at his birth. For he shall be great in the sight of the Lord, and shall drink neither wine nor strong drink; and he shall be filled with the Holy Ghost, even from his mother's womb. (Luke 1:14–15)*

He did say that! Zacharias thought. Suddenly, he realized, *This is an angel! That's how he knew about us!*

Zacharias was fascinated. The angel said they would have a son who would be great in the sight of the Lord. How wonderful!

The angel continued,

> *And many of the children of Israel shall he turn to the Lord their God. And he shall go before him in the spirit and power of Elias, to turn the hearts of the fathers to the children, and the disobedient to the wisdom of the just; to make ready a people prepared for the Lord. (Luke 1:16–17)*

Their son would be named John, and he would be used to bring many people of Israel to God. Zacharias was amazed.

CHAPTER 3

Doubt Creeps In

But wait, Zacharias thought. Uncertainty began to cloud his mind. *How can this be? Elisabeth and I are too old*. He asked the angel,

> *Whereby shall I know this? for I am an old man, and my wife well stricken in years. (Luke 1:18)*

As soon as Zacharias said those words, he regretted them. The angel's expression suddenly changed. He replied,

> *I am Gabriel, that stand in the presence of God; and am sent to speak unto thee, and to shew thee these glad tidings. And, behold, thou shalt be dumb, and not able to speak, until the day that these things shall be performed, because thou believest not my words, which shall be fulfilled in their season. (Luke 1:19–20)*

Zacharias realized his error, but too late. How could he doubt God like that? He knew the Scriptures. He remembered what the angel had said to Abraham long ago, when his wife Sarah could not have a child:

> *Is any thing too hard for the LORD? At the time appointed I will return unto thee, according to the time of life, and Sarah shall have a son. (Genesis 18:14)*

Zacharias and Elisabeth knew God had given Abraham and Sarah a miracle child in their old age, and they believed God could do the same for them.

Now their prayers had been answered. And how did Zacharias reply? Unbelief! Zacharias tried to apologize. He moved his lips. No sound.

The angel disappeared.

The temple was quiet once again. Zacharias stood alone, watching the candles flicker, their lights dancing on the wall. An angel had appeared to him and said God had answered their prayer for a child. Yet he had questioned God's Word and God's ability. And he, a priest!

"Is any thing too hard for the LORD?" Of course not!

Yet his muteness was a blessing, in a way. It was proof that God's promise still stood. Zacharias watched the incense rise toward heaven, just as prayers went up to heaven, and God heard them! A son! And he would be a great prophet! God had answered their prayers mightily!

Zacharias felt so unworthy to serve such a great God, yet so blessed. A tear rolled down his cheek, followed by another. And another. He wiped his face with a sleeve. He asked God to forgive him for his lack of faith and thanked God for his grace.

CHAPTER 4

The People Wait Outside

And the people waited for Zacharias, and marvelled that he tarried so long in the temple. (Luke 1:21)

Zacharias stood, thinking about the angel's visit. It had all happened so fast. Did it really happen? He tried to speak out loud. Silence.

Suddenly, he thought, *How long have I been here?* He needed to leave!

Outside the temple, people had finished their time of prayer and stood waiting for Zacharias, talking among themselves.

"What's taking him so long?"

"Do you think he's okay?"

"I wonder if he's become ill."

As they wondered, Zacharias appeared in the doorway. They sighed with relief. "Zacharias, are you okay?" they asked.

Zacharias could not speak, so he tried to explain with gestures what had happened.

> *And when he came out, he could not speak unto them: and they perceived that he had seen a vision in the temple: for he beckoned unto them, and remained speechless. (Luke 1:22)*

"Zacharias," they asked, "what happened? What did you see?"

Zacharias thought about the angel and his words and Zacharias' response of unbelief. He couldn't describe what had happened. He simply waved and smiled, then left. They stood and wondered.

Later, Zacharias thought about the angel's words:

> *And many of the children of Israel shall he turn to the Lord their God. (Luke 1:16)*

Those words made sense. He felt many people in Israel did not act like God was real. They went to the temple and read Scriptures and prayed, but they didn't seem to take God seriously in how they lived their lives.

Yet his son, whom God called John, would be used to bring them to faith in God. *What a wonderful God we serve,* Zacharias thought.

CHAPTER 5

Elisabeth and Zacharias

And it came to pass, that, as soon as the days of his ministration were accomplished, he departed to his own house. (Luke 1:23)

Elisabeth heard the door of the house open.

"Is that you, sweetheart?" she called from the back.

No answer.

"Zacharias?"

Silence.

Zacharias should be coming about now, she thought. Yet if it were him, why did he not answer? Curious and a little fearful, Elisabeth went to the doorway that led from the kitchen to the house's main room. She peeked around the corner and saw her husband. Relieved, she walked up and embraced him.

"Honey, I'm so glad you're home."

Zacharias didn't answer. He hugged and kissed her, then smiled.

"Honey, why aren't you talking?" Elisabeth pulled back from his hold.

Zacharias let go of her and walked to a table. He sat down, picked up a pen and paper, and gestured for her to come. He then began to write as Elisabeth looked over his shoulder.

"An...angel...appeared...to...me," Elisabeth read aloud, resting her hands on his shoulders. "Really, honey?" she asked, amazed.

He looked up and nodded, then continued. Her eyes were glued to the page.

"He...said...our...prayers...were...heard." Her voice rose with excitement, "And...we...would...have...a...*son!* Zacharias, that's wonderful!" Elisabeth exclaimed tearfully, hugging his neck. "We had prayed so long for a child!"

Zacharias leaned his head against hers and patted her arm, then held up an index finger in a "Wait, there's more" gesture. He continued to write while Elisabeth watched in eager anticipation.

"The...angel...said...the...boy's...name...would... be...John," Elisabeth read. "And...he...would...be... great...in...the...sight...of...the...Lord...and...turn... many...people...in...Israel...to...God. Oh Zacharias," she said, hugging him as he stood, "thank the Lord! We're going to have a son, and he will be a prophet of the Lord."

Suddenly, she backed off. "But why can't you speak?"

Zacharias rolled his eyes sheepishly. He sat back down, picked up the pen again, and wrote. He handed her the paper. She read it.

"Oh," was all she said.

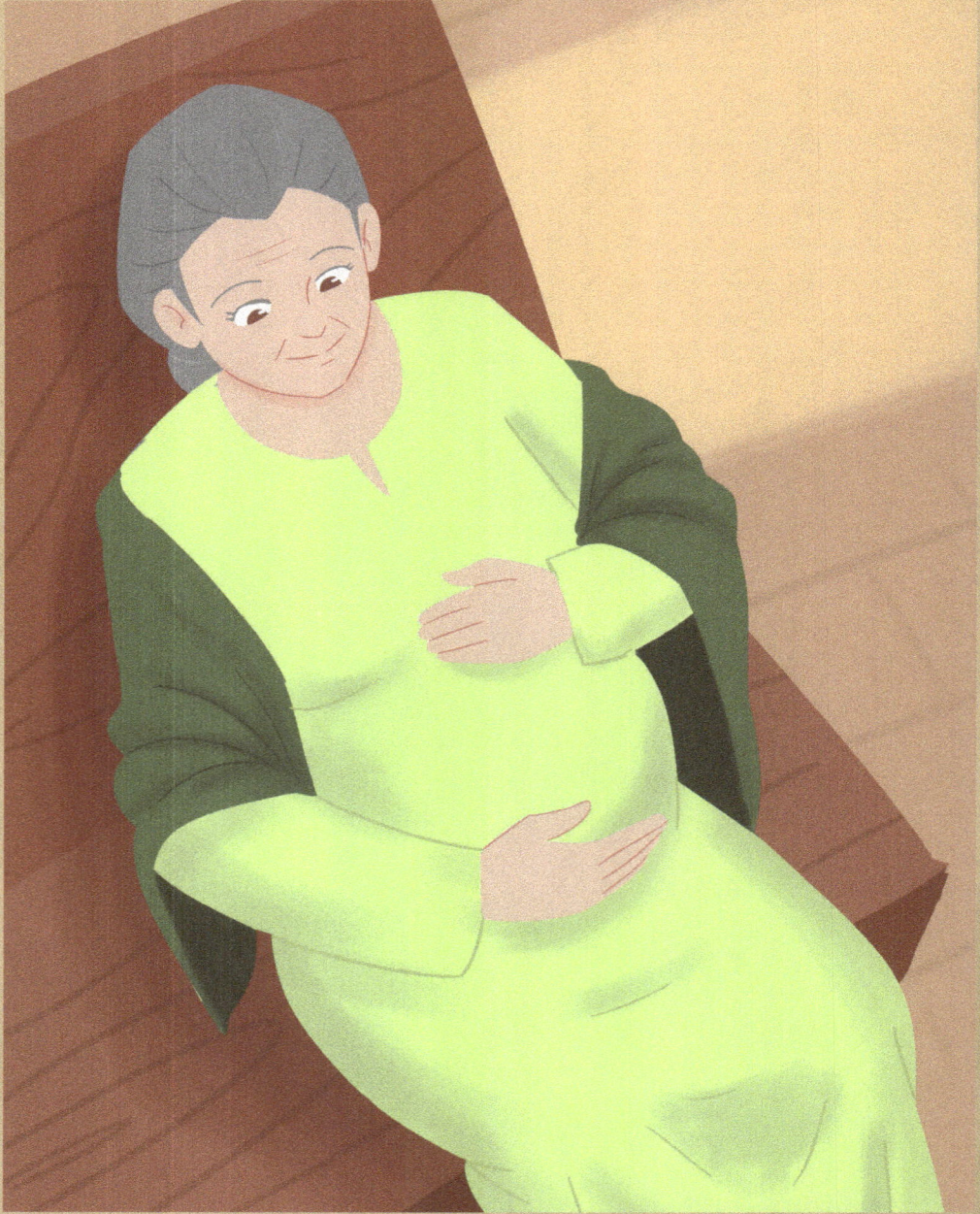

CHAPTER 6

Elisabeth with Child

And after those days his wife Elisabeth conceived, and hid herself five months, saying, Thus hath the Lord dealt with me in the days wherein he looked on me, to take away my reproach among men. (Luke 1:24–25)

Elisabeth sat and pondered with her hand on her growing stomach. She and Zacharias had prayed and hoped for a child for so long. Now they were old enough to be grandparents, but still no child.

Until now.

God had answered at last! And this son would be a prophet of God, great in the sight of the Lord.

Elisabeth was so thankful. She had not yet told anyone, but she would. Soon. She would tell her neighbors and cousins. They would be glad.

Elisabeth had heard the way people talked. Not being able to bear a child was painful enough. Why did people have to talk about it and be hurtful?

Didn't they read their Scriptures? Sarah was unable to have a child until God blessed her. So was Rebekah. So was Rachel. So was Hannah. And now, Elisabeth thought joyfully, so was she.

Elisabeth felt a movement inside her. She inhaled reflexively, then relaxed and smiled, patting her stomach.

"Moving around in there, John?" she asked. "Soon you'll be here with us."

CHAPTER 7

Mary

And in the sixth month the angel Gabriel was sent from God unto a city of Galilee, named Nazareth, To a virgin espoused to a man whose name was Joseph, of the house of David; and the virgin's name was Mary. (Luke 1:26–27)

Mary hummed as she bustled about the kitchen. There is no one in the world like a young lady in love, and Mary was very much in love.

Marriages at that time were usually arranged between families. Yet Mary's parents had told her they prayed for wisdom to choose a good husband for her.

When they told her about Joseph's family and that both sets of parents believed he was the one for her, she was thrilled. Mary knew Joseph. He was a carpenter. He was a gentleman, worked hard, and loved the Lord. She could also tell he was interested in her.

Mary gathered the ingredients for a honey cake. Joseph would stop by later. Honey cake was his favorite. As Mary prepared, she thought about their many conversations.

After they became engaged, they talked about what it would be like when they married. These conversations were always fun. They talked often about having children. Mary thought about strong young boys doing carpentry like their father or girls cooking and making clothes.

As Mary prepared the honey cake and looked forward to married life, she suddenly felt uneasy. Someone else was in the room with her.

CHAPTER 8

Gabriel Appears to Mary

She turned to see a large, powerful-looking man standing in the middle of the kitchen. He wore a dazzling white garment. Mary backed away.

"Who are you?" she asked fearfully. The man spoke:

> *Hail, thou that art highly favoured, the Lord is with thee: blessed art thou among women. (Luke 1:28)*

Who is this man? Mary thought. *And what does he mean, that I'm highly favoured?*

> *And when she saw him, she was troubled at his saying, and cast in her mind what manner of salutation this should be. (Luke 1:29)*

The man spoke again:

> *Fear not, Mary: for thou hast found favour with God. And, behold, thou shalt conceive in thy womb, and bring forth a son, and shalt call his name JESUS.*
>
> *He shall be great, and shall be called the Son of the Highest: and the Lord God shall give unto him the throne of his father David:*
>
> *And he shall reign over the house of Jacob for ever; and of his kingdom there shall be no end. (Luke 1:30–33)*

Favor with God? This is an angel! Mary realized. *He even knows my name, and he said I would have a son who would be a king! How could that be?*

Joseph was not from a royal family. Nor was she. She also would never want another man, even from a royal family. Her true love was Joseph.

> Mary asked the angel, *How shall this be, seeing I know not a man? (Luke 1:34)*

The angel replied,

> *The Holy Ghost shall come upon thee, and the power of the Highest shall overshadow thee: therefore also that holy thing which shall be born of thee shall be called the Son of God. (Luke 1:35)*

CHAPTER 9

The Mother of the Messiah

Did I hear that right? Mary thought. *The Son of God?* She could hardly believe her ears. Then she realized, *The angel was talking about the MESSIAH!*

God had promised that the Redeemer would come one day. The first promise was in the garden of Eden when God told the serpent,

> *And I will put enmity between thee and*
> *the woman, and between thy seed and her seed;*
> *it shall bruise thy head, and thou shalt bruise*
> *his heel. (Genesis 3:15)*

Since that time, faithful people had waited for the promised Redeemer. They knew he would be born of a virgin. The Scripture said so:

> *Behold, a virgin shall conceive, and bear*
> *a son, and shall call his name Immanuel.*
> *(Isaiah 7:14)*

Now he was coming, and Mary would be his mother! Mary was amazed!

The angel continued,

> And, behold, thy cousin Elisabeth, she hath also conceived a son in her old age: and this is the sixth month with her, who was called barren. (Luke 1:36)

Elisabeth and Zacharias! A baby! Mary's cousin and Zacharias had always wanted a child but could not have any. Yet now they would have a son! Mary was overwhelmed. The angel then told her,

> For with God nothing shall be impossible. (Luke 1:37)

Mary stood in silence as the angel's words sank in. She had never thought she would be the one for God to choose. Yet now the angel looked at her with piercing eyes, as if waiting for her answer. Would she agree to this? Mary knew what the answer should be.

> And Mary said, Behold the handmaid of the Lord; be it unto me according to thy word. (Luke 1:38)

Suddenly, the angel was gone. She looked around. Everything was the same as it had been—all quiet, the dishes on the shelf, the late afternoon sun shining through the window. Did all this really happen? Did she really consent to be the mother of the Messiah?

The angel had said so many things. It was so vivid, so real. It was no dream. She would be the Messiah's mother, and Joseph would be the stepfather!

Joseph! She suddenly realized. Joseph would be here soon! She had to finish the cake! As Mary bustled about, mixing ingredients and warming up the oven, she thought about how Joseph would react to the news.

He would be thrilled, she thought.

CHAPTER 10

Mary Tells Joseph

Now the birth of Jesus Christ was on this wise: When as his mother Mary was espoused to Joseph, before they came together, she was found with child of the Holy Ghost. (Matthew 1:18)

The freshly baked honey cake cooled on the counter. The late afternoon sun brightened up the kitchen. Mary heard a familiar knock at the door. She opened it to Joseph's smiling face.

"Hi, sweetheart," she said.

"How are you, honey?" he asked, stepping through the door.

"Great. How was work?" she asked as he walked past her.

"Fine," he replied, holding his tool belt. "We did house repairs and furniture. How about you?"

"Well," Mary said, taking a deep breath and saying a quick prayer, "I've got wonderful news."

Joseph turned to look at her. "Great. About what?" he asked, sitting down and laying the tool belt on the floor.

"Well, it's about both of us," Mary replied, still seeing the angel in her mind's eye. "I almost don't know where to start."

Joseph shrugged. "How about the beginning?"

"Okay, well, I was in the kitchen this afternoon making your favorite honey cake, which, by the way, is finished. Do you want some?"

"It can wait, sweetheart," Joseph said. "I want to hear this news."

"Well," she said, joining him at the table, "I was in the kitchen and suddenly felt like someone else was there. I turned around and saw this great big man dressed all in white."

"A man?" Joseph asked, surprised. "What did he want? What did he say?"

"Joseph, honey," she said, "I believe it was an angel."

"An angel?"

"Yes, honey. He told me I was highly favored and blessed among women."

"What does that mean?"

"He also said I had found favor with God, and I would conceive and have a son, and his name would be Jesus."

"He said *what*?"

"Not only that, Joseph. He said this child would be the Son of God. And I realized he was telling me I would be mother to the Messiah!"

Joseph sat quietly as her words sank in.

"Then," she continued, "he said my cousin Elisabeth is pregnant in her sixth month. And you know how she and Zacharias had always wanted a child."

"They're old enough to be grandparents," Joseph replied. "And they're going to have a child?"

"Yes, honey, and do you realize what this means? The Saviour we've waited for so long is coming. God has chosen me to be his mother and you to be his stepfather."

Mary saw his expression suddenly fall.

"What happened then?" he asked.

"I told him I would do what God wanted me to do. Joseph, honey, isn't this wonderful?"

Mary could tell by his expression that he didn't think it was wonderful.

"Joseph, what's wrong? Aren't you happy?"

"No. I mean, yes," Joseph said distractedly. "I, uh, have to go."

He got up from the table.

"Darling, are you okay?" Mary was perplexed.

"Yes, I'm fine," Joseph stammered. "I just have a lot of work to do tomorrow."

He walked to the door and opened it.

"Joseph?"

He turned to her in the doorway. "Yes, Mary?"

She held out the tool belt. "Don't forget this."

"Oh. Thanks." He took the belt, opened the door, and walked out into the balmy, late-afternoon air.

She watched his retreating figure. "Bye, Joseph. Love you."

"Bye, Mary. Love you too," he replied over his shoulder, not looking at her.

Mary watched his silhouette become smaller as he walked away. She folded her arms and leaned in the doorway. *He is not happy*, she thought.

CHAPTER 11

The Angel Appears to Joseph

Then Joseph her husband, being a just man, and not willing to make her a public example, was minded to put her away privily. (Matthew 1:19)

A dazzling array of stars filled the midnight sky over Nazareth. The clusters of small buildings glowed under the moon's warm light. An occasional lamp shone through a window here and there, providing a golden contrast to the dark silhouettes of the structures.

The citizens of the quiet town of Nazareth lay asleep in their beds, enjoying a much-needed rest to prepare for the next day's activities.

Not all of them. One young carpenter lay wide awake, staring at the ceiling.

Stepfather to the Messiah? Me? Joseph thought anxiously.

Joseph knew the Scriptures about the Messiah's coming:

> *Therefore the Lord himself shall give you*
> *a sign; Behold, a virgin shall conceive, and*
> *bear a son, and shall call his name Immanuel.*
> *(Isaiah 7:14)*

Joseph also had put his trust in the coming Redeemer, and he wanted to please God in his life. Even Mary's parents told him they felt he was God's choice for their daughter.

Yet as he drifted into an uneasy sleep, troubled thoughts circled through his mind. *I'm just a carpenter. I can't be the Messiah's stepfather. But God chose Mary to be his mother. Does that mean I should break up with her? I don't want to break up. I love Mary. But I'm just a carpenter…*

> *But while he thought on these things,*
> *behold, the angel of the Lord appeared unto him*
> *in a dream, (Matthew 1:20)*

Suddenly, Joseph sat up. Someone else was in the room! Joseph saw a large, powerful-looking man dressed in a shining white garment.

The man spoke:

> *Joseph, thou son of David, fear not to*
> *take unto thee Mary thy wife: for that which is*
> *conceived in her is of the Holy Ghost.*
> *And she shall bring forth a son, and thou*
> *shalt call his name JESUS: for he shall save his*
> *people from their sins. (Matthew 1:20–21)*

Who is this man? Joseph thought? *How does he know what I'm thinking? How does he know about Mary? He even said she would have a son, and His name would be Jesus and…*

Suddenly, Joseph realized, *That's what Mary was talking about!* At that instant, as if on cue, the man was gone. The room was dark and quiet once again.

But Joseph could still see the man and hear his words in his mind: *Joseph, thou son of David, fear not to take unto thee Mary thy wife:*

That was an angel! Fearsome to look at, but his words were calm and reassuring. It was just like the visit from the angel that Mary had described.

The angel even called Joseph a son of David. Joseph knew the Messiah would come from David's family line:

> *For unto us a child is born, unto us a son is given: and the government shall be upon his shoulder: and his name shall be called Wonderful, Counsellor, The mighty God, The everlasting Father, The Prince of Peace.*
>
> *Of the increase of his government and peace there shall be no end, upon the throne of David, and upon his kingdom, to order it, and to establish it with judgment and with justice from henceforth even for ever. The zeal of the LORD of hosts will perform this. (Isaiah 9:6–7)*

Joseph sat up and leaned against the wall. So the prophet's words were about to come true! *A virgin will give birth to the Son of God. She would have a husband, and no one would know, at least not at first, that the child was not*

his. *The husband would come from David's line. And he and Mary were the couple God chose.*

Joseph still didn't feel worthy to be stepfather to the Messiah. Yet God had chosen him, worthy or not, and the angel had answered every question and objection Joseph had.

Joseph looked out the window. The sun was rising above the hills, a fresh, beautiful light.

How long was I awake? thought Joseph. He didn't know how long he had slept, but he was amazed at how refreshed he felt.

He washed, read his morning Scripture, prayed, and thanked the Lord for giving him the assurance he needed.

I will be stepfather to the Saviour, Joseph thought. *And his name will be Jesus. And God will give me the help I need.*

Joseph dressed, gathered his tool belt, packed a lunch, and headed for work. But first, he had to make an important stop.

CHAPTER 12

Mary and Joseph

Then Joseph being raised from sleep did as the angel of the Lord had bidden him, and took unto him his wife: And knew her not till she had brought forth her firstborn son: and he called his name JESUS. (Matthew 1:24-25)

The sun rose over Nazareth. Mary looked out the window. The sky was a cheerful blue, but her mood was cloudy. When she told Joseph what had happened, he obviously wasn't happy. She didn't know why.

Mary recalled a favorite Scripture in the psalms. It helped her when she faced a problem she didn't know how to handle:

Trust in the LORD, and do good;
(Psalm 37:3)

Mary had trusted God to send a Saviour who would redeem them from sin. She also, though not perfect, strived to do good. Mary prayed quietly for the Lord to help her and Joseph. Now she could only think to trust the Lord to work in this matter.

Just as she finished praying, she heard a knock at the door. She recognized it immediately. *Joseph!* She opened the door.

"Hi," he said with a wide smile.

"Hi," she replied cautiously.

"I had a dream last night," he told her.

Mary's eyes widened a little. "About what?"

"An angel told me not to be afraid to marry you."

"An *angel?*"

"The angel appeared to me last night, sweetheart. Just like you had described, big and fearsome. But he called me a son of David and said the child was conceived of the Holy Ghost and you would have a Son."

Mary collapsed against the doorframe in relief.

"Oh, thank you, Lord," she whispered.

"I'm sorry about the less-than-happy reaction yesterday."

"It's okay, honey," Mary replied, gracious as usual. "God knew you needed that assurance. That's why He sent the angel."

"But I feel so unworthy to do this," Joseph said.

"So do I," Mary replied. "But it's not about how worthy we are, but how great our God is."

"The angel even told me what the baby's name would be," Joseph added with a grin.

Mary smiled.

"Jesus," they said in unison.

CHAPTER 13

Mary Visits Elisabeth

And Mary arose in those days, and went into the hill country with haste, into a city of Juda; And entered into the house of Zacharias, and saluted Elisabeth. (Luke 1:39–40)

Mary looked forward to seeing Elisabeth. She wanted to tell her about the angel's visits to her and Joseph.

She arrived at the house as Zacharias walked out the front door. She called his name.

"Zacharias!"

Zacharias looked her way and hesitated, not recognizing her at first. Then a huge smile crossed his leathery face. He walked out to her, arms outstretched. She met him in the yard. They exchanged a warm embrace.

"Zacharias, I heard the news about Elisabeth. Where is she?"

The elderly priest beamed and nodded. He motioned for her to follow him into the house.

Why doesn't he say anything? Mary thought.

Zacharias disappeared into the back, then re-appeared with Elisabeth, her large belly showing and her face aglow.

Mary beamed. "Elisabeth! It's wonderful to see you!"

The older woman suddenly put her hand on her protruding belly, smiled, and said,

> Blessed art thou among women, and blessed is the fruit of thy womb.
>
> And whence is this to me, that the mother of my Lord should come to me?
>
> For, lo, as soon as the voice of thy salutation sounded in mine ears, the babe leaped in my womb for joy.
>
> And blessed is she that believed: for there shall be a performance of those things which were told her from the Lord. (Luke 1:42–45)

Elisabeth knew Mary would be mother to the Messiah! Mary was amazed! The two women embraced.

"Sit down, Mary, please. Do you want something to eat?"

"Let me tell you what happened first," Mary replied.

"Please do," Elisabeth said.

The three sat down.

"Why doesn't Zacharias talk?" Mary asked.

"I'll tell you in a little while," Elisabeth replied. "Go ahead with your story."

"Okay. One day, I was making Joseph a honey cake," Mary started. "He always stopped by after work. Suddenly, I felt like someone was behind me. I turned around and saw this angel standing there."

Elisabeth and Zacharias listened intently.

"He was big and fearsome-looking, but he told me not to be afraid," she continued.

Zacharias nodded enthusiastically and looked at Elisabeth, pointing to Mary in agreement.

"He told me I would give birth to a Son and would call His name Jesus, and He would reign over the house of Jacob for ever. The angel also said you were pregnant in your sixth month, and we knew how much you two had wanted a child. I wanted to come and see."

"Jesus," Elisabeth said. "The name Jesus means 'God is salvation.' What a wonderful name. What did Joseph say when you told him?"

"At first, he wasn't happy. He told me later he had not thought he'd be a worthy stepfather to the Messiah."

Elisabeth disagreed. "I think Joseph would be a fine stepfather."

"But an angel appeared to him that night," Mary continued, "and told him not to be afraid to marry me. He even told Joseph the baby's name."

"The Lord is so good," Elisabeth said.

"So what happened with you?" Mary inquired.

"Actually, it happened with Zacharias," Elisabeth replied. "He was in the temple offering incense. An angel appeared and said God had heard our prayers for a child, and we would have a son, and his name would be John."

"John?" Mary asked.

"Yes," Elisabeth replied. "Not only that, John would be a prophet, and God would use him to bring many people in Israel to God. So not only will we have a son, but he will be a prophet who will be great in the sight of the Lord."

"I'm so happy for you," Mary said. "But why can't Zacharias speak?"

"Well," Elisabeth said, "someone had a bit of a faith crisis. When the angel said Zacharias and I would have a son, he asked how could that happen when we're so old. I guess someone forgot that nothing is impossible with God."

She gave Zacharias a smile and a pat on the knee. "Then the angel told him that because of his lack of faith, Zacharias would not be able to speak until the day these things are fulfilled."

Mary saw Zacharias shake his head sheepishly. She looked at Elisabeth.

"Oh," was all she could think to say.

"That's what I said," Elisabeth replied with a slight smile.

> *And Mary abode with her about three months, and returned to her own house. (Luke 1:56)*

CHAPTER 14

"His Name Is John!"

Now Elisabeth's full time came that she should be delivered; and she brought forth a son. And her neighbors and her cousins heard how the Lord had shewed great mercy upon her; and they rejoiced with her. (Luke 1:57–58)

Three ladies knocked at the door. Zacharias barely had time to open it before they peppered him with excited questions.

"Zacharias, how is Elisabeth?"

"How is the baby?"

"Is it a boy or a girl?"

"Do you have a name picked out?"

"Can we see them?"

Zacharias smiled and beckoned them to enter and sit down. He held up his index finger in a "wait a minute" gesture, then retreated toward the back of the house.

Soon Elisabeth appeared, holding a bundle.

The ladies jumped up from their seats and let out a chorus of "oohs" and "aahs" as they surrounded Elisabeth and the baby.

"So how's the proud father?" one of them asked.

He smiled but could not answer.

"Do you know why he can't talk?" she asked.

"We think it will clear up soon," Elisabeth said, dodging the question as she winked at Zacharias.

> *And it came to pass, that on the eighth day they came to circumcise the child; and they called him Zacharias, after the name of his father. (Luke 1:59)*

People gathered at the home of Zacharias and Elisabeth for the ceremony of the circumcision of their newborn son.

"What a beautiful child," they exclaimed one after another.

One of Elisabeth's cousins smiled as she held the boy. "Hello, little one," she cooed.

The priests asked for the ceremony to start.

"Now the baby's name is Zacharias, right?"

Zacharias and Elisabeth shook their heads.

> *And his mother answered and said, Not so; but he shall be called John. And they said unto her, There is none of thy kindred that is called by this name. And they made signs to his father, how he would have him called. And he asked for a writing table, and wrote, saying, His name is John. And they marvelled all. (Luke 1:60–63)*

Zacharias turned the writing table to the priests. "His…name…is…John," they read in unison. "John?" they asked curiously.

> *And his mouth was opened immediately, and his tongue loosed, and he spake, and praised God. (Luke 1:64)*

"Yes, John," Zacharias said, then he stopped. He could speak!

"Yes!" he exclaimed. "The boy's name is John!" Zacharias repeated, excited at the sound of his own voice. "Thank you, Lord. You are so gracious and wonderful. You are so worthy of our praise!"

"Zacharias, you can speak!" their friends said in amazement.

"Yes, I can, and the baby's name is John!"

"Then John it is," said the priests, smiling.

CHAPTER 15

From Nazareth to Bethlehem

> *And it came to pass in those days, that there went out a decree from Caesar Augustus, that all the world should be taxed.*
>
> *(And this taxing was first made when Cyrenius was governor of Syria.)*
>
> *And all went to be taxed, every one into his own city.*
>
> *And Joseph also went up from Galilee, out of the city of Nazareth, into Judaea, unto the city of David, which is called Bethlehem; (because he was of the house and lineage of David.)*
>
> *To be taxed with Mary his espoused wife, being great with child. (Luke 2:1–5)*

The journey from Nazareth to Bethlehem was not easy. The terrain was sometimes hilly and rough, and dangerous animals were known to roam in the wilderness. Yet Mary and Joseph could see God's hand of protection. Their journey, though long, had been relatively trouble-free.

Once in Bethlehem, Mary and Joseph would register for the tax that Caesar Augustus had levied. Joseph could not go alone. Mary had to be with him, pregnant or not.

Joseph looked back at her, sitting on the donkey, bumping along as they walked, holding her large stomach.

"How are you doing, sweetheart?" Joseph asked. He had asked that question many times since they had started from Nazareth.

Mary smiled tiredly. "I'm fine, dear." She was still her usual cheerful self.

"Do you need to stop and rest?"

"Not yet."

As Joseph walked, he thought about the Scripture that foretold the Messiah's birth in Bethlehem:

> But thou, Bethlehem Ephratah, though thou be little among the thousands of Judah, yet out of thee shall he come forth unto me that is to be ruler in Israel; whose goings forth have been from of old, from everlasting. (Micah 5:2)

Thinking of this Scripture gave Joseph peace of mind. God was always good for his word. If God's word said Jesus would be born in Bethlehem, then it would happen.

As the angel had said,

> For with God nothing shall be impossible. (Luke 1:37)

Still, Joseph found himself praying often along the way.

CHAPTER 16

No Room in the Inn

And so it was, that, while they were there,
the days were accomplished that she should be
delivered. (Luke 2:6)

Evening faded into night. Joseph and Mary arrived at the inn in Bethlehem. Joseph tied up the donkey in the front. He let Mary down, then walked her to the front door. He opened it to let her in, then followed.

The innkeeper and his wife stood leaning over the front counter.

"We'd like a room," Joseph asked.

"I'm sorry, but we're full," the innkeeper replied.

"But my wife is due to have a baby," Joseph said. "We came from Nazareth."

"Looks like the baby is coming soon, too," the innkeeper's wife added. "Here, honey, have a seat," she said, offering Mary a chair.

"Thank you," Mary replied as she sat.

"If we had a room," the innkeeper said, "I'd give it to you, but everything in town is full because of Caesar's tax."

Joseph stood there frustrated, not knowing what to do. "Lord, please help," he prayed quietly.

After several uncomfortable moments, the innkeeper's wife spoke up. "Honey," she offered, "what about the stable?"

She didn't like the idea, but they had nothing else and the time was late, so the couple didn't have much choice.

"I know this isn't great," she told them. "But we can make it decent for you."

Mary summoned her strength. "That would be fine, thank you." She smiled, looking at Joseph.

"Okay, sweetheart," the older woman assured her. "We'll get right on it."

"How much will this cost?" Joseph asked tiredly.

"To put you up in a stable? Nothing," the innkeeper replied. "I'm embarrassed we can't do any better."

"Thank you for doing this," Joseph replied. He could feel his mood improving. "It means a lot."

The innkeeper disappeared into a back room and returned with blankets and lanterns.

"Follow me," he told the young couple.

"Honey," he called to his wife as he exited, "see what you can cook up for these people, okay? They're probably starved."

"Okay, dear," she replied, leaving the room.

Turning to Joseph, he added, "That's on the house, too."

Joseph smiled back. "Thank you. We are hungry. And I can pay."

"I'm sure you can, but we won't take it. Call it a baby gift."

CHAPTER 17

The Saviour is Born

*And she brought forth her firstborn son,
and wrapped him in swaddling clothes, and
laid him in a manger; because there was no
room for them in the inn. (Luke 2:7)*

Mary and Joseph leaned over the tiny sleeping figure in the hay. Here he was. The Messiah, the Son of God, the Saviour of the world.

"Isn't it amazing, honey," Joseph said, "how God worked out so many details. He let us be married, and chose you to be the Messiah's mother."

"And you to be stepfather," Mary reminded him.

"And how he allowed Zacharias and Elisabeth to have a son, and the angel told you about her being with child," Joseph added.

"And God told her about me being the mother of the Messiah," Mary said.

"Even you being here because of Caesar's tax was God's work," Joseph added. "I wonder if Caesar will ever learn he fulfilled Scripture."

"The Lord got us safely here from Nazareth, and the innkeeper and his wife fed us and put us up for free," Mary commented. "Now here we are."

"What do you think it will be like, raising a child who is the Son of God?" Joseph asked.

"We don't know," Mary replied, "but the Lord got us this far. He'll give us the help we need."

CHAPTER 18

Shepherds in the Field

And there were in the same country shepherds abiding in the field, keeping watch over their flock by night. (Luke 2:8)

Stars and constellations spread out as far as the eye could see in the deep-blue sky outside Bethlehem. A full moon smiled warmly on the hills. Torches burning about the flock's perimeter cast an orange hue onto the backs of the sheep. The air was cool but comfortable. The young shepherd loved being here.

Suddenly, his ears perked. A soft but painful cry. The young shepherd recognized it right away. He grabbed his staff and moved swiftly toward the noise. He had no time to lose.

The young shepherd quickly reached the edge of the flock and saw a large figure disappearing into the darkness, its tail swinging.

A lion!

"Stop!" he ordered.

The lion turned toward the young shepherd, his trophy hanging helplessly in his jaws. The young shepherd moved forward, raised the staff with both hands, and smashed it onto the lion's head. The lion roared in pain and dropped the lamb from its mouth.

Now the bleeding, angry lion turned to the young shepherd with a snarl. The young man dropped his staff, unholstered his dagger, and braced for the lion's attack.

The lion advanced and jumped. The young shepherd stiff-armed him with his left and grabbed the bottom of the lion's mane. He plunged the dagger into the lion's chest.

The lion roared again painfully, swiping at the young shepherd with a paw as he fell to the ground. The young shepherd held the mane tightly with a strong arm as the lion twisted, attempting to bite and claw.

Soon the lion began to lose strength from loss of blood. His attempts to fight became weak and meaningless. Eventually, he collapsed and lay quietly, his body heaving with each breath.

The young shepherd let go of the mane, picked up the lamb, and stood over the fallen lion. The lion turned to the young shepherd with a look of defeat, dropped its head, closed its eyes, and breathed its last.

The boy re-holstered his imaginary dagger and turned. "Now, Goliath, you're next!" he warned the also-imaginary giant, pointing his finger. He drew his sling and quoted his famous ancestor's words:

> Thou comest to me with a sword, and with a spear, and with a shield: but I come to thee in the name of the LORD of hosts, the God of the armies of Israel, whom thou hast defied.
> This day will the LORD deliver thee into mine hand; and I will smite thee, and take thine

head from thee; and I will give the carcases of the host of the Philistines this day unto the fowls of the air, and to the wild beasts of the earth; that all the earth may know that there is a God in Israel.

And all this assembly shall know that the LORD saveth not with sword and spear: for the battle is the LORD's, and he will give you into our hands. (1 Samuel 17:45–47)

The shepherd watched his son pretend to be David, as he had done many times before. First, he would kill the lion and rescue the little lamb. Then he would turn to Goliath and kill him with a stone slung to his head, just as David had done long ago. The boy even memorized what David had said. He enjoyed this game immensely, and his father was never tired of watching him.

All was quiet on this night. Some of the shepherds were walking among the sheep or standing watch at the edge of the flock. One shepherd played a flute, the soft, cheerful music floating among the hills.

Some of the shepherds had brought their sons to the field on this night. The men were glad for extra help, and the boys felt very grown up working in the field at night.

Meanwhile, the lion had been killed and the lamb rescued once again. The shepherd watched as his son pulled a sling from his belt, dropped a stone into the pouch, and spun the weapon in his hand. Goliath was about to get his.

Suddenly, a light shone above. It lit up the sky and the field brighter than the midday sun. All the shepherds turned their heads upward in fear. The flute music stopped.

The boy dropped his sling. The stone bounced out. He was no longer David, a brave young shepherd rescuing a helpless lamb, or a soon-to-be hero, coming to his nation's rescue. He was a terrified eight-year-old running into his father's arms.

CHAPTER 19

The Angel Visits the Shepherds

The shepherd held his young son tightly as he and the other shepherds shielded their eyes from the light's piercing rays.

A fearsome-looking man appeared in the sky. The shepherds gaped, frozen in terror. The man spoke, a strong, booming voice:

> *Fear not: for, behold, I bring you good tidings of great joy, which shall be to all people.*
> *For unto you is born this day in the city of David a Saviour, which is Christ the Lord.*
> *And this shall be a sign unto you; Ye shall find the babe wrapped in swaddling clothes, lying in a manger. (Luke 2:10–12)*

As the shepherds watched, a huge array of angels appeared in the sky.

> *And suddenly there was with the angel a multitude of the heavenly host praising God, and*

saying, Glory to God in the highest, and on earth
peace, good will toward men. (Luke 2:13–14)

The shepherds gazed at the huge company of angels. The sight of them praising God was amazing beyond words. As they watched, the dazzling light that filled the sky became dimmer. The angels faded from sight.

Soon all was quiet once more. The night sky was again dark, the stars glittering across it. It was as if nothing had happened. But the shepherds knew something had happened, something wonderful.

> *And it came to pass, as the angels were gone away from them into heaven, the shepherds said one to another, Let us now go even unto Bethlehem, and see this thing which is come to pass, which the Lord hath made known unto us. (Luke 2:15)*

The shepherds started talking all over each other in a mix of excited voices.

"Father, those were angels!"

"Did you see how big they were?"

"I've never seen anything like it!"

"And the angel said the Saviour had been born!"

"Yes, in Bethlehem, the city of David!"

"The promise we've waited so long for is come true!"

"We must go to Bethlehem right away!"

"Yes, the angel said we'd find him wrapped in swaddling clothes!"

"And lying in a manger!"

"Father," the shepherd boy exclaimed, "let's go see the Saviour."

The shepherds gathered together to go to Bethlehem.

"How will we find him in the middle of the night?" one shepherd asked.

"The angel said, 'Ye shall find the babe,'" a boy said confidently. "God will help us find Him."

The group left a small contingent to keep the sheep as they hurried to Bethlehem.

CHAPTER 20

Finding the Saviour

And they came with haste, and found Mary, and Joseph, and the babe lying in a manger. (Luke 2:16)

The innkeeper stood at the counter, trying to add up the night's income. The numbers didn't match. His wife walked in, sensing his frustration.

"What's the matter, honey?" she asked.

"I'm rechecking my math. The numbers aren't adding up," he scowled.

"Why don't you leave it alone for now? It's late, and you're tired."

"Good idea," he conceded. "How is the family out there?"

"Mary and Joseph are fine," she reported, "they have a boy, his name is Jesus, and he's perfect. By the way, do you remember that extra manger you made a month ago?"

"Yes. Why?"

"It makes a great crib. We put straw into it. Jesus is in it now."

Suddenly, they heard several loud knocks at the door. They looked at each other. *Who could that be this late at night?*

The innkeeper walked to the door and opened it. A group of shepherds stood, men and boys, obviously excited.

"Can I help you?" he asked.

One of the men spoke. "I know this will sound crazy, but we're looking for a baby who was just born."

Almost immediately the boys piped in, talking over the man and over each other. The man was trying to make himself heard over all of them and control his own excitement.

The innkeeper tried to listen to them all at the same time. It wasn't easy.

"We were watching the sheep…"

"And we were out in the field…"

"And there was this big angel in the sky…"

"The sky lit up like it was day…"

"And he said he brought us good tidings of great joy…"

"Did you see it?"

"And there were all these angels!"

"He said the Saviour was born in the city of David!"

"The angel called Him Christ the Lord…"

"There were so many angels in the sky…"

"You had to see it!"

The innkeeper pieced together the story.

Then one boy said, "He said the baby would have swaddling clothes and be lying in a manger."

The innkeeper looked at his wife. Swaddling clothes? A manger? They were talking about the baby in the stable!

That baby Jesus was their long-awaited Messiah!

"Follow us," he told them.

The innkeeper led them outside to the stable. He opened the door quietly.

"Joseph? Mary? Can we come in?"

"Come on in," Joseph replied in a loud whisper.

The innkeeper led the group back to where Mary and Joseph sat resting. Blankets had been hung for privacy. The lanterns gave off a quiet, serene light.

"Is the baby here?" a shepherd boy piped in.

"Shhh!" his father admonished, his finger to his mouth.

Mary smiled and pointed to the manger nearby, where a newborn boy lay sleeping, wrapped in swaddling clothes on a bed of straw. The group circled him with awe and wonder.

The tiny form rustled occasionally as he slept.

"Can we touch him?" one of the boys asked.

Mary nodded.

The boys played with Jesus' tiny fingers and lightly touched his face. Time seemed to stand still as the group gazed at the sleeping Saviour.

One boy touched Jesus' hand. The baby Jesus, his eyes still closed, opened his hand and held the older boy's finger in a gentle grip.

"Look, Dad, he has my finger!" the boy whispered, beaming. He moved his finger back and forth gently as the Saviour enclosed it.

Joseph asked them, "How did you know to come here?"

"We were out in the field watching sheep," one of the men replied, "when this angel suddenly appeared in the sky!"

Joseph and Mary listened intently.

"We were all scared, but then he told us not to be afraid!"

Mary and Joseph exchanged smiles. It sounded like the visits from the angel they had seen.

"He said he had good tidings of great joy for all people," the shepherd continued. "He said the Saviour, Christ the Lord, was born in the city of David, and we would find him wrapped in swaddling clothes, lying in a manger."

"We wanted to see the Saviour. We figured since God told us about Him, God would let us find Him. We came into town and saw the lights on at the inn. We knocked at the door, and the innkeeper brought us here."

Joseph was amazed. God even planned for them not to find a room in the inn. Jesus would have to be born in a place where the shepherds would know where to look for him.

"The lights were on because I was working on the books," the innkeeper said. "God used the lights to help you—and us—find the Saviour."

After a time, one of the men spoke. "Come on, boys. Let's go. We'll let the family rest."

The boys pulled reluctantly away from the manger, their eyes riveted on the sleeping Jesus.

"Okay, Father, but we've got to tell people that the Saviour has been born!" a shepherd boy replied urgently.

"We will!" his father assured him.

And when they had seen it, they made known abroad the saying which was told them concerning this child.

And all they that heard it wondered at those things which were told them by the shepherds. (Luke 2:17–18)

The innkeeper, his family, and the shepherds left. Mary and Joseph sat back on the straw. She was amazed at how God worked so many things out. She was happy and blessed to serve such a wonderful God.

But Mary kept all these things, and pondered them in her heart. (Luke 2:19)

Joseph thought quietly about the privilege he had been given: to be stepfather to the Son of God. He did not know what lay ahead for him and Mary, but he was confident that God would give them the grace and help they needed.

CHAPTER 21

Is the Saviour Your Saviour?

The story of Jesus did not end here. Jesus grew up into adulthood. He healed sick people, cast out devils, raised the dead, did miracles, and "*…went about doing good,*" (*Acts 10:38*).

Most importantly, he allowed himself to be falsely arrested, tried, convicted, sentenced, and executed by a slow and brutal death: crucifixion. Yet he was buried and rose again on the third day, victorious.

He appeared to his disciples and remained on earth for forty days, then ascended into heaven, leaving them the promise that he would one day return.

Jesus also forgave sins and saved souls. Sinners came to him to be forgiven their sins, and he forgave and saved them.

Jesus still does that today. None of us have seen Jesus, since he ascended into heaven long ago. Yet we have the Bible to assure us that he is God the Son, his death did pay for our sins, he was buried and rose again, and he forgives sins and saves souls for those who receive him.

After Jesus arose, he appeared to his disciples, but Thomas was not among them. The other disciples told him that they had seen the Lord; but Doubting Thomas, as he is sometimes called, did not believe until he had seen Jesus personally.

Jesus told Thomas, "*Thomas, because thou hast seen me, thou hast believed: blessed are they that have not seen, and yet have believed.*" *(John 20:29)*

The second part of that verse is for believers in Jesus today. We have never seen or heard Jesus, but we believe in him based on what the Bible says. In that sense, the story of Jesus still goes on.

That said, is the Saviour *your* Saviour?

The angel told the shepherds, "*For unto you is born this day in the city of David a Saviour, which is Christ the Lord.*" *(Luke 2:11)*

We need a Saviour because we have done wrong things. The Bible calls those wrong things sins, and our sins have separated us from God. "*For all have sinned, and come short of the glory of God;*" *(Romans 3:23)*

Our sins have also condemned us to death: "*For the wages of sin is death;*" *(Romans 6:23)*. Finally, our sins have condemned us to eternal hell: "*And death and hell were cast into the lake of fire. This is the second death.*" *(Revelation 20:14)*.

Yet God loved us and sent His Son, Jesus, to die in our place: "*But God commendeth his love toward us, in that, while we were yet sinners, Christ died for us.*" *(Romans 5:8)*

Jesus took the punishment for all our sins by dying on the cross! "*Who* [Jesus] *his own self bare our sins* [all of them] *in his own body on the tree*," *(1 Peter 2:24)*

Jesus was also buried, but He did not stay in the grave. He rose from the dead and is alive today: "*I am he that liveth, and was dead; and, behold, I am alive for evermore, Amen;*" *(Revelation 1:18)*.

Christmas is a time of giving and receiving gifts. God wants to give people the gift of eternal life and a home in heaven. "*But as many as received him, to them gave he power to become the sons of God, even to them that believe on his name.*" *(John 1:12)*

Jesus is *the* Saviour. He becomes *your* personal Saviour when you turn from sin and receive him. When you do, he forgives you all your sins, saves you, makes you a child of God, and gives you a home in heaven.

Church does not save you. Nor do baptism or good deeds. Yet Jesus saves you and gets you to heaven when you trust completely in him.

You may know the Christmas hymn, "O Little Town of Bethlehem." Verse 3 is about receiving him as your personal Saviour. It says,

> No ear can hear His coming, but in this
> world of sin, Where meek souls will receive
> Him still, the dear Christ enters in.

("O Little Town of Bethlehem," Phillips Brooks and Louis H. Redner, 1868)

Romans 10:13–14 says, *"For whosoever shall call upon the name of the Lord shall be saved. How then shall they call on him in whom they have not believed?"*

You may go to church and celebrate Christmas, but have you ever received the Lord Jesus as your personal Saviour? Are you 100 percent sure from the Bible that you will go to heaven? If not, you could receive him right now. You could call on him like this, if you mean it:

> *Lord Jesus, I'm sorry for all my sins. Please forgive me. Thank you for dying for me. Come into my heart and life and be my personal Saviour. I'm trusting completely in you to get me to heaven. Thank you for saving me.*

If you have just called on Jesus like that, trusting in him entirely to forgive you your sins and get you to heaven, you have assurance from the Bible that he saved you. The Scripture says anyone who calls upon Jesus *"shall* [not might] *be saved."* The Bible does not lie. Isn't eternal life a wonderful Christmas gift?

After you receive Jesus as your personal Saviour, find a church where the Word of God is preached and where people are told how to be saved. A church like this is a place where you can learn more about your Saviour and grow in your Christian life.

ABOUT THE AUTHOR

Brian Miller is a retired Cleveland police officer, having served for thirty-three years. He also serves as a chaplain for the Cleveland Division of Police. He and Debbie, his wife of twenty-six years, make their home in Greater Cleveland. They have two adult children.

Brian is also the author of *Strength unto the Battle*, a book of essays for police officers.

Printed in the USA
CPSIA information can be obtained
at www.ICGtesting.com
JSHW011912290924
70601JS00011B/38